PRE-COLUMBIAN DESIGN

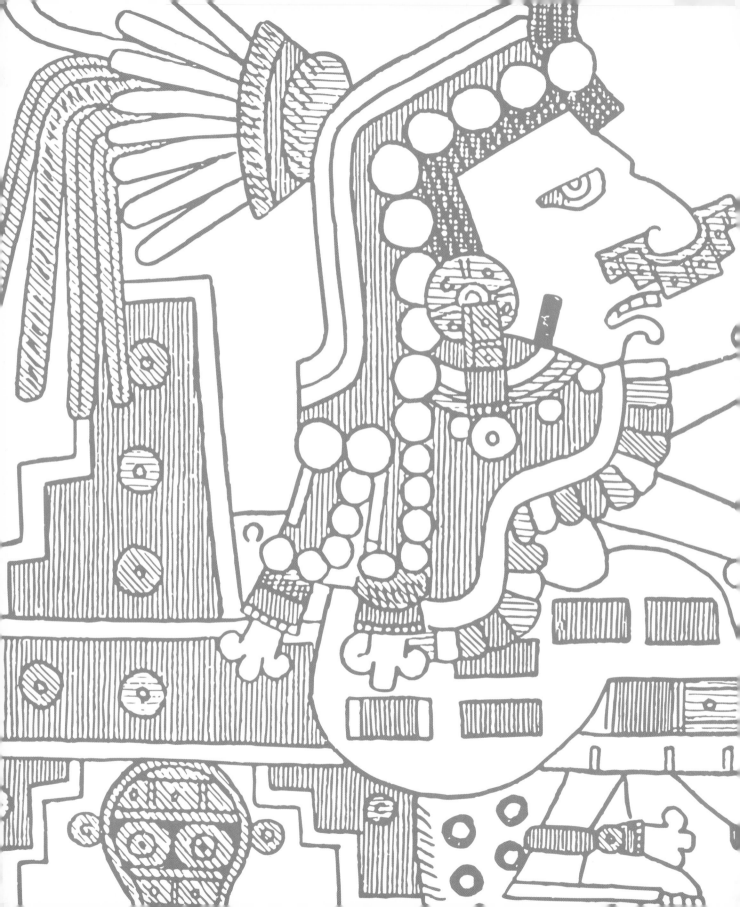

PRE-COLUMBIAN DESIGN

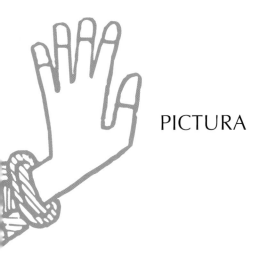

PICTURA

DOVER PUBLICATIONS, INC. | Mineola, New York

By Alan Weller.
Designed by Joel Waldrep.

Pre-Columbian Design is a new work, first published by Dover Publications, Inc.,
in 2008.

For permission to use more than ten images, please contact:
Permissions Department
Dover Publications, Inc.
31 East 2nd Street
Mineola, NY 11501
rights@doverpublications.com

The CD-ROM file names correspond to the images in the book. All of the artwork
stored on the CD-ROM can be imported directly into a wide range of design and
word-processing programs on either Windows or Macintosh platforms. No further
installation is necessary.

ISBN 10: 0-486-99751-0
ISBN 13: 978-0-486-99751-3
Manufactured in the United States of America
Dover Publications, Inc., 31 East 2nd Street, Mineola, NY 11501
www.doverpublications.com

005

006

008

009

012

015

017

018

020

021

023

024

025

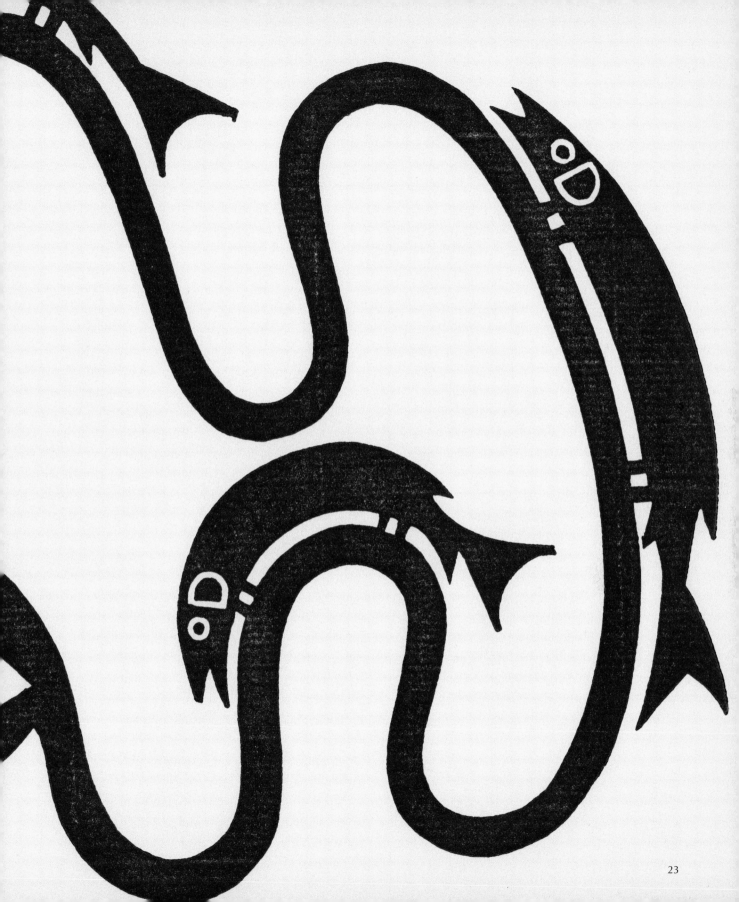

033

034

037

038

039

36

040

041

042 background

043–050

051

053

054

058

059

061

062

064

065

066

068

069

070

071 background

072

073

076

077

52

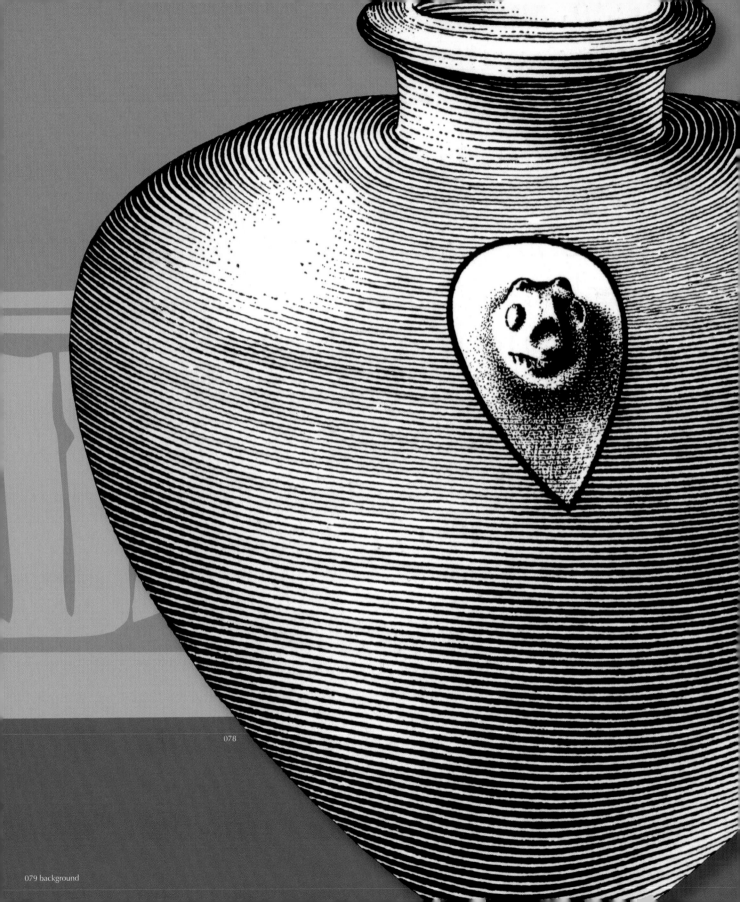

080

081

082

084

085

088

089

090

094 background

095

097

098

100

102

103

65

104

105

106 background

107

108

109

114

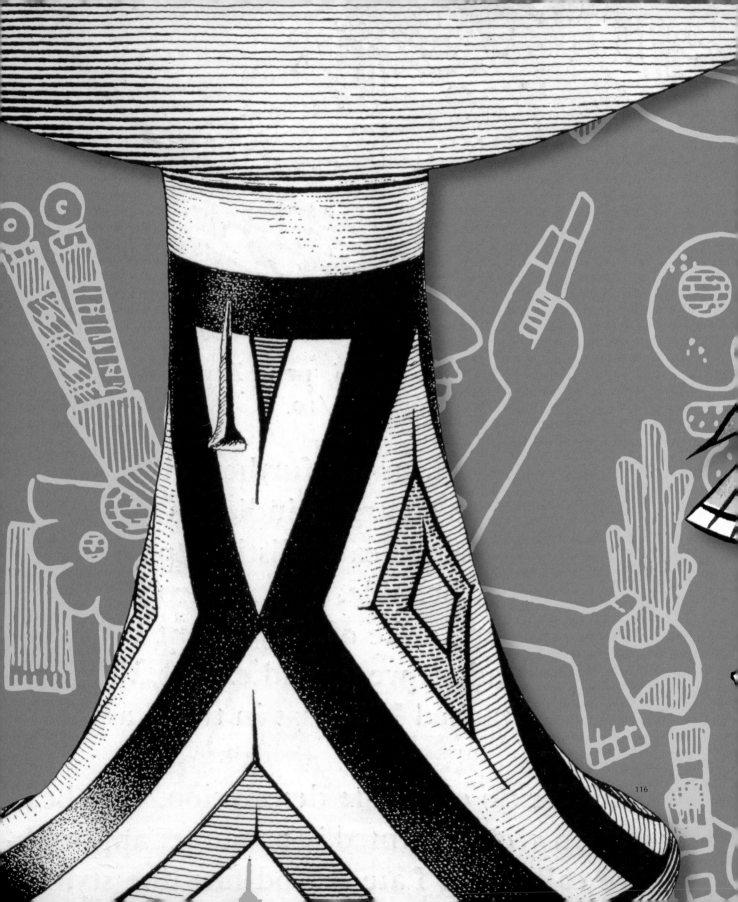

117

119

120

122

123

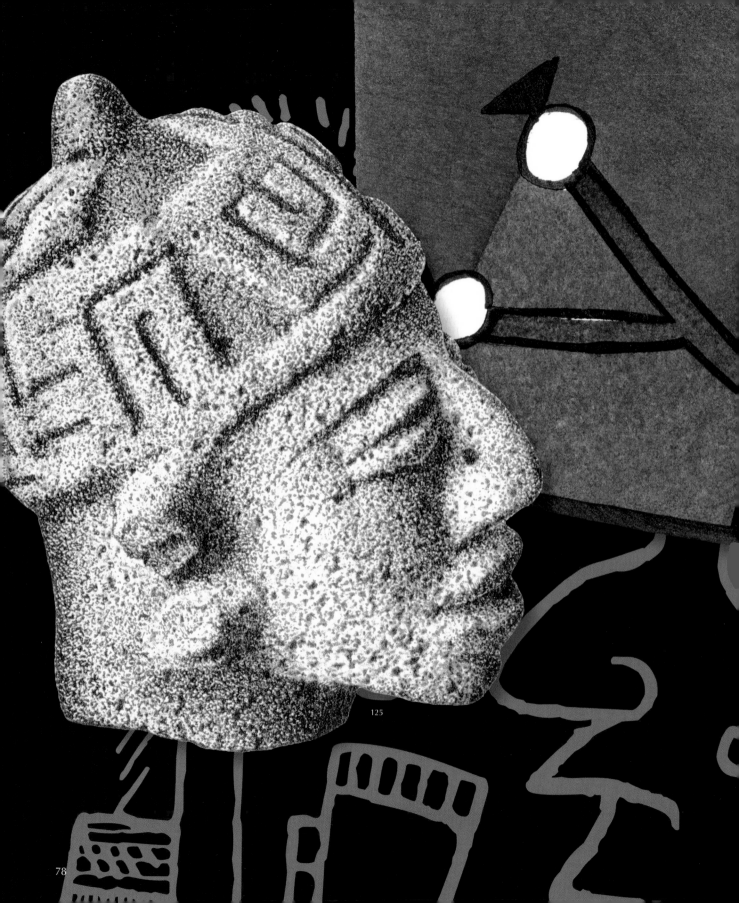

125

78

126

128

131

132

133 background

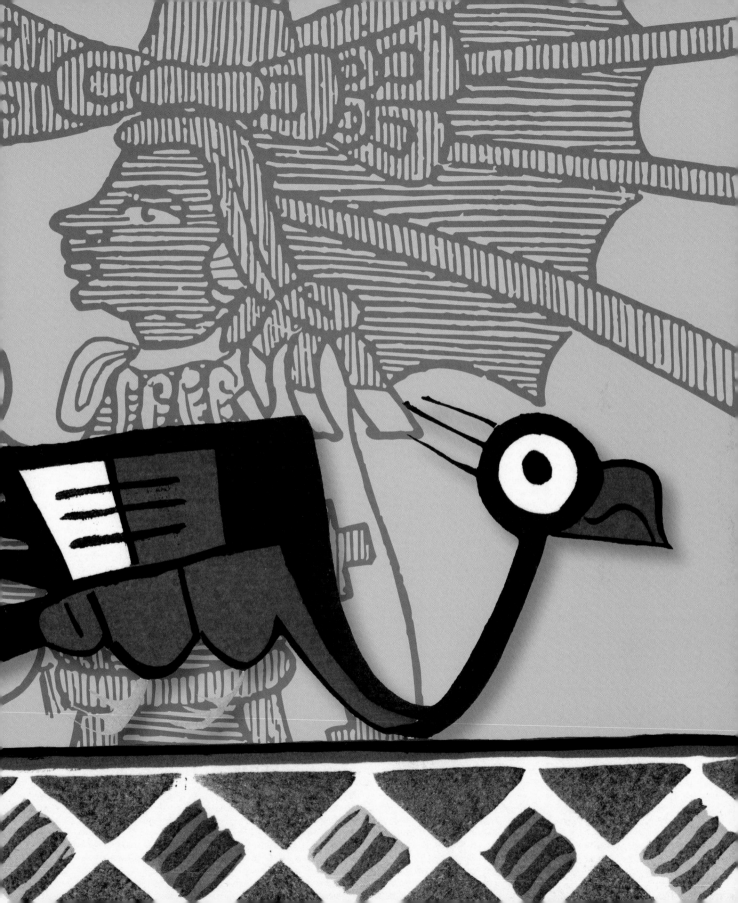

134

135

137

138

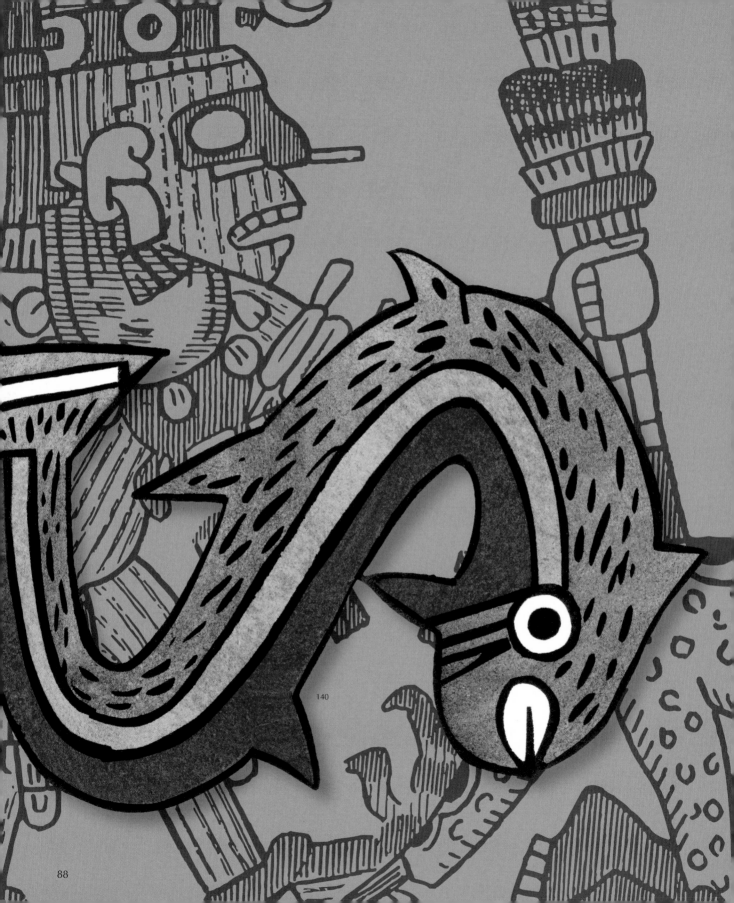

141

143

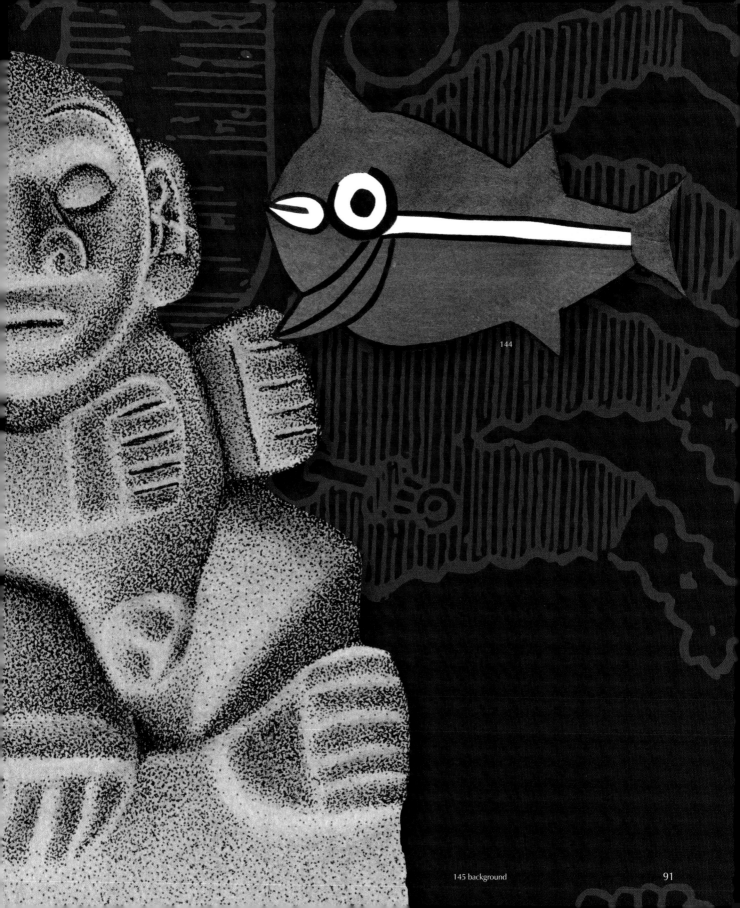

144

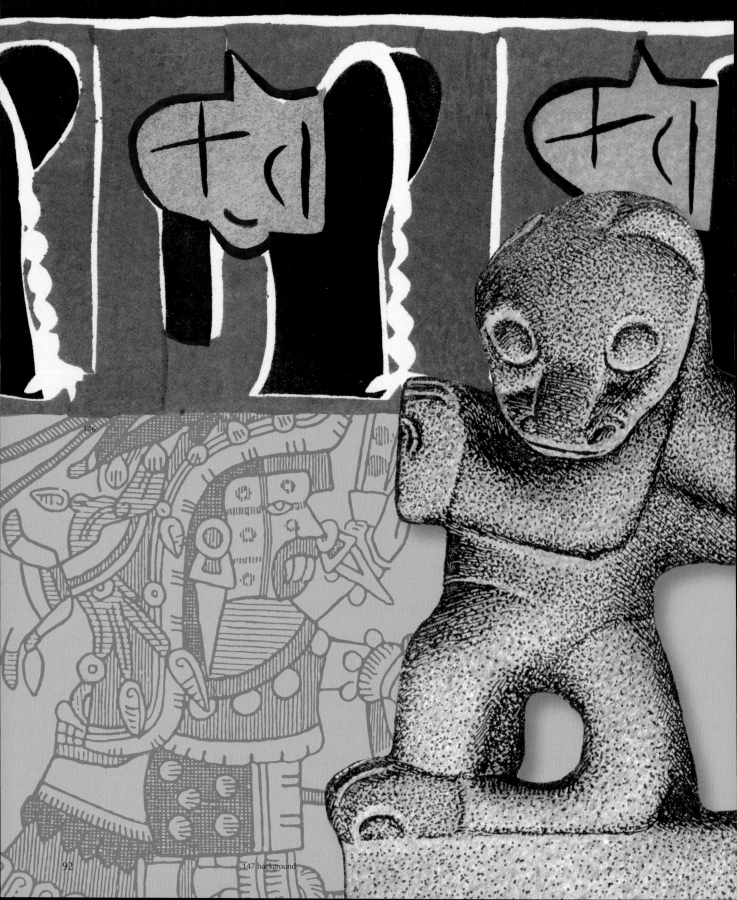

146

147 background

148

149

150

152

153

155

158

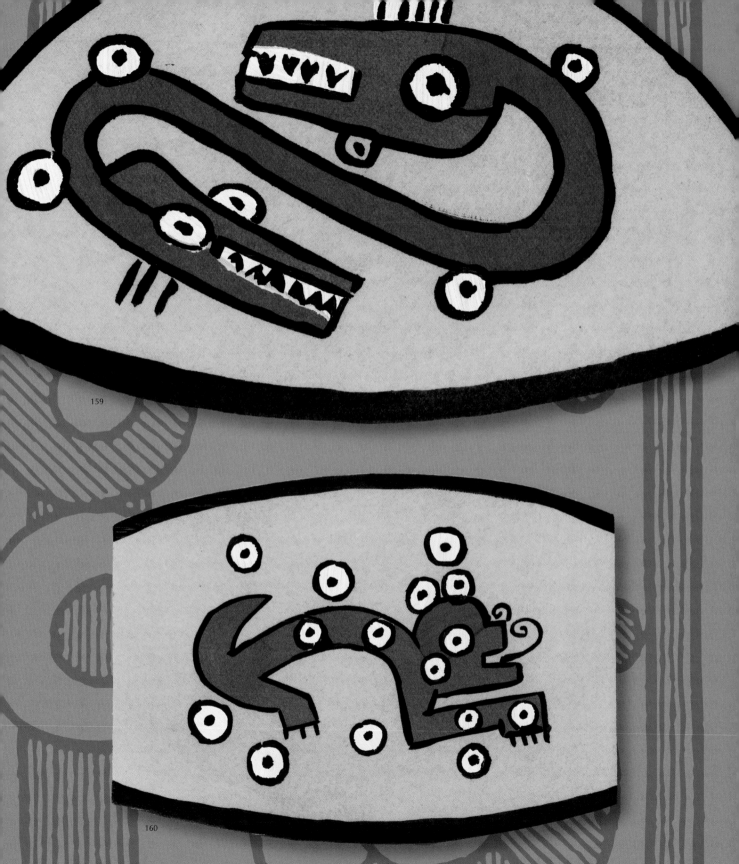

159

160

162

163

164

166

168

169

171 background

170

172

173

174

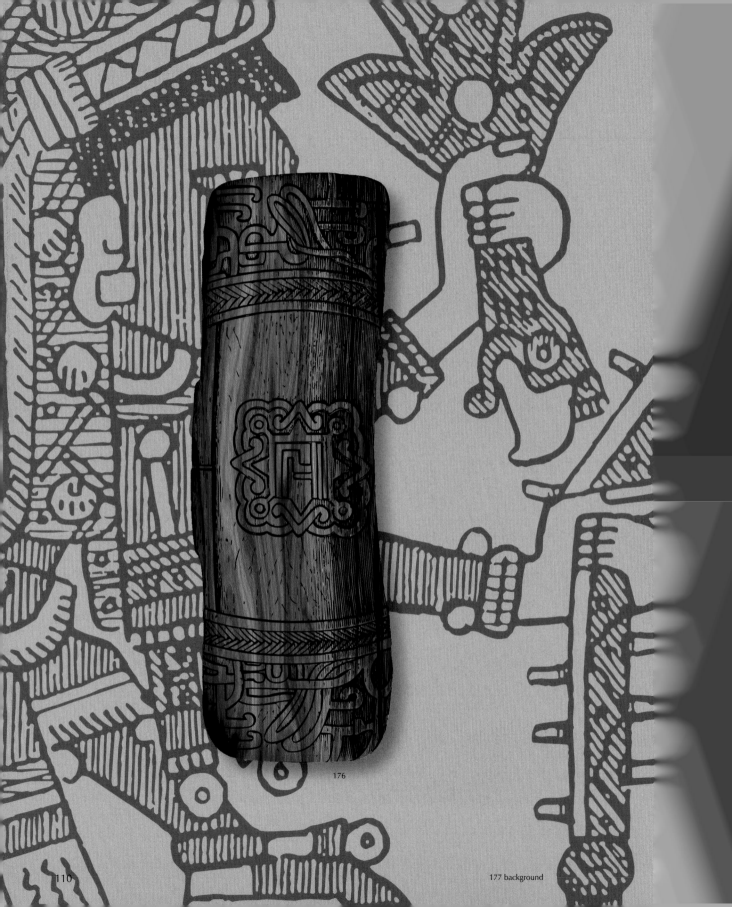

176

177 background

179

180 background

182

183

185

187

186 background

188

189

193

194

195

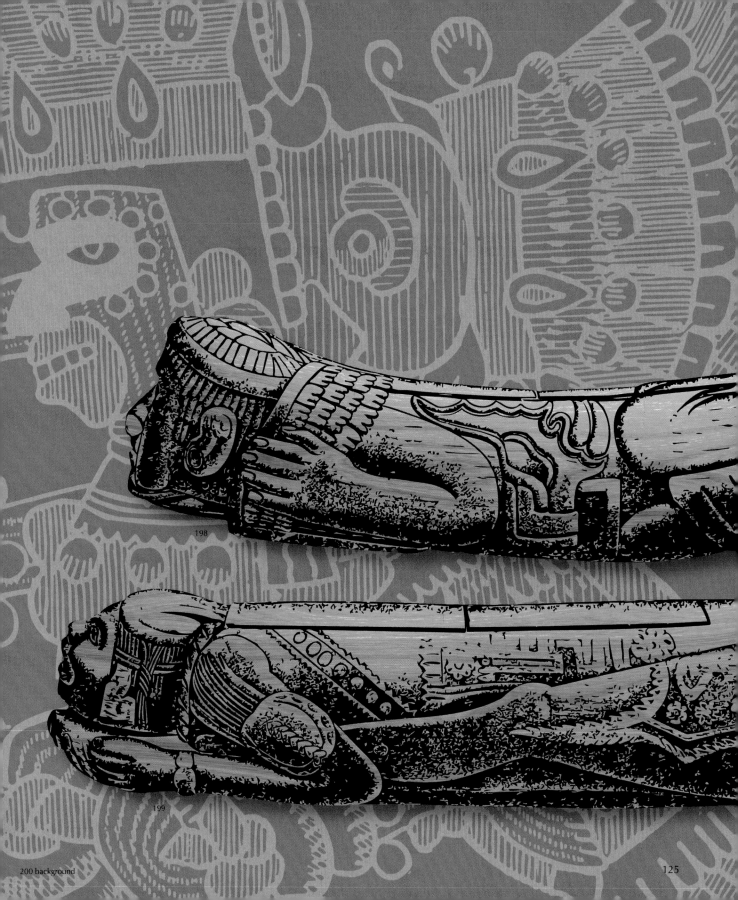

198

199

201

202

203 background